ORIGINAL
SQUISHMALLOWS™

ORIGINAL SQUISHMALLOWS™

RADIATE POSITIVITY

Andrews McMeel
PUBLISHING®

CONTENTS

"THE ONLY THING THAT WILL MAKE YOU HAPPY IS BEING HAPPY WITH WHO YOU ARE, AND NOT WHO PEOPLE THINK YOU ARE."

—Goldie Hawn

INTRODUCTION

Hello! We're the Squishmallows. We love spending time together, and we're so glad that you've decided to chill with us. Being a 'Mallow means keeping things positive, having fun, and taking care of each other—but that doesn't mean life is always easy! There are new twists, turns, challenges, and opportunities every day. Whether you're stressed, facing something that scares you, or just feeling bogged down, we've got you. That's why we've put together a little advice that will help you live more like a 'Mallow. That means focusing on the good, spreading joy, and being kind to yourself, even when life gets tough.

This book is all about taking care of a very special person—YOU! Because just like every 'Mallow has a unique story, we know that you are a one-of-a-kind individual with your own talents and interests. The thing we want you to know is that we're here for you. You have dreams and ambitions, and the best way to achieve them is by believing in yourself and showing love and gratitude every day—no matter what other people think.

We can't wait to see how you like our book. Remember: You're already awesome just by being yourself. It's up to you to build yourself up, so that you can share your sparkle with the world. **BE KIND. BE HAPPY. BE YOU!**

A FEW OF OUR FAVORITE THINGS

Things that make Squishmallows
happy can make you happy too!

DRESSING UP

PLAYING SPORTS

PRACTICING MINDFULNESS

MOVIES!

HULA HOOPING

MAKING MUSIC

BEING ARTISTIC

LEARNING SOMETHING NEW

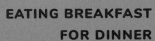

**EATING BREAKFAST
FOR DINNER**

A WEEKEND at MY FAVORITE BEACH

SQUAD
Goals

One of the best parts of being a 'Mallow is that we all belong to squads made of Squishmallows we love. There's nothing better than spending time with close friends and family, right? They are always there to cheer us on and pick us up when we fall down. The happiest people have strong relationships. Just like besties Safiyah and Lola or dynamic duo Rudy and Daxxon, you deserve friends who recognize just how special you are. The best way to find your squad is by pursuing your passions and being active in your community. Having true friends can make the world easier to handle—so expand your squad, and shower them with love!

YOUR FRIENDS ARE LIKE ROCKS

THEY HELP YOU THROUGH HARD TIMES.

"TRY TO BE A RAINBOW
iN SOMEONE'S CLOUD."

—Maya Angelou

BE GENEROUS. This doesn't mean buying presents, but everyone appreciates a compliment or a call just because. The more you can show people you care about them, the more it will strengthen your relationships. Here are five ways you can be generous without spending any extra dough!

1. Tell a new friend something that you like about them.

2. Share something you made. Winston is famous for making culinary delights—what's your signature dish?

3. Make a playlist of songs that remind you of your squad and share it!

4. If a friend is getting ready for something important, like an interview or a presentation, help them prep! Hans is always helping Lola run lines for her auditions.

5. Grab your phone and record a voice memo for someone you care about. Tell them to play it back whenever they're doubting their awesomeness.

"FRIENDSHIP IS BORN AT THE MOMENT WHEN ONE PERSON SAYS TO ANOTHER 'WHAT! YOU TOO? I THOUGHT I WAS THE ONLY ONE.'"

—C. S. Lewis

TRY A NEW ACTIVITY—
EVEN IF IT SEEMS SCARY!

You may not be great at first, but you might make
new friends who are learning too. Look for something
that meets regularly so you can keep coming
back and building exciting new relationships.

YOUR FUNNY VIBE
ATTRACTS YOUR
FUNNY TRIBE.

Hey, what do you think is the best way to strike up a convo? We think it's by asking lots of questions! People loooove to talk about themselves, so ask where they're from, where they got their shoes, or if there are any super-cool, exclusive collector's items they love to hunt for. ☺

A LITTLE COMPETITION CAN ADD EXCITEMENT TO YOUR WEEK.

Find a sport or a game that gets your heart pumping, and do it in a group! Organizing a group activity is a great excuse to get together with friends you haven't seen in a while, and joining a new group is the perfect way to meet new people. Avery's made so many friends on his Squishmallows rugby team, while Wanda and Danny can share their love of games at game night!

JUST LIKE A
pineapple,
YOU MIGHT BE ROUGH
AROUND THE EDGES AT TIMES,
BUT SHARE THE
SWEETNESS
THAT'S
INSIDE YOU.

SHOW US THAT SMILE!

Smiling can actually make you feel better—when you smile, your body releases hormones that reduce pain and stress. PLUS, it makes the people around you more comfortable and relaxed.

Your smile is infectious.

NOT EVERYONE HAS TO LIKE YOU.
NOT EVERYONE HAS TASTE!

IF YOU DON'T GET ALONG WITH SOMEONE, THAT'S OK—but don't let them walk all over you. Stand up for yourself, and if you see someone being mistreated, stand up for them too! Do a gut check—if something feels wrong, there's probably a reason. Trust those instincts.

BELIEVE IN YOURSELF—
YOUR FRIENDS
BELIEVE IN YOU!

Say Yes.

When you're getting to know new people and they invite you to do something, you might be nervous about making a good impression—but GO FOR IT. It shows people that you're excited to be in their squad!

"MOST PEOPLE
ARE NICE
WHEN YOU
FINALLY
SEE THEM."

—Harper Lee

TAKE ONE SMALL STEP TO HELP OTHERS—

like volunteering once a month. It'll be easy for you, and it could make a big difference for someone else. And choose something that will make you feel good too!

If you love flowers, see if your neighborhood has a community garden!

 If you're into animals, see if your local shelter needs someone to walk dogs or foster cats!

If stories are your jam, you can read to people in need!

Chanel is a pastry chef who volunteers at the local food pantry and teaches baking classes.

Harrison is a counselor for Big/Little 'Mallows and brings the little 'Mallows on hikes.

"THE BEST WAY TO CHEER YOURSELF is TO TRY TO CHEER SOMEONE ELSE UP."

—Mark Twain

Make a personalized photo album or card for someone in your squad just to say that you love them. Draw, paint, or stamp on a blank card, or find materials, like washi tape, pretty papers, or old puzzle pieces, and glue them onto your card to make a one-of-a-kind embellished design that could ONLY come from you.

Find out what your friend's favorite song is. Pick out a lyric, make a drawing of it, and give it to them on their birthday. Or whenever they need your support.

Honestly, getting a homemade gift feels more meaningful and distinctive. Whether you give your creation to someone you haven't seen in a while or someone you see every day, we bet it'll make them smile.

IT'S A SQUISH HUNT
Can you find?

1. Muffin
2. Canoe
3. Bendy straw
4. Sailboat
5. Candle
6. Hat
7. Oar
8. Nail
9. Tack
10. Fortune cookie
11. Golf club
12. Carrot
13. Hammer
14. Flag
15. Pitcher
16. Jack the Black Cat
17. Toothbrush

Solution on page 116

EMBRACE
Positivity

Sometimes people ask, "Hey Squishmallows, how come you all seem so happy?" Well, the first step to that is focusing on the GOOD moments in our lives! This doesn't mean pretending nothing bad happens, but maintaining a positive outlook will help you regain your balance faster. Practicing gratitude and positivity can reduce negative thoughts and help you succeed in school or work. Good vibes also help open the door for better relationships with the people around you! So why not give it a try?

I'M NOT LION WHEN

I SAY YOU'RE

Roar-Some!

PRACTICE POSITIVE SELF-TALK—
remember to congratulate yourself on a job well done,
or say, "Way to go, me!" when you achieve a goal!
Putting a positive spin on things can help you feel
more confident about yourself, motivate you to move
past obstacles, and help you spread joy to others.

"GRATITUDE is
the
CLOSEST THING TO
BEAUTY MANIFESTED
IN AN EMOTION."

—Mindy Kaling

SAY "THANK YOU" TO THE PEOPLE WHO HELP IN YOUR COMMUNITY—bus drivers, shopkeepers, service workers, teachers, or colleagues.

When you're thanking someone, take a pause and be specific. Instead of just saying, "Thanks, Angie," try: "Thank you for sharing your peanut butter brownies with me! It was so nice that you thought of me—plus, they were delicious!" Being specific will help you take notice of the wonderful things in your life to be grateful for.

DON'T EVER MISS A CHANCE TO SAY "THANK YOU"!

YOU DESERVE SUGAR, SPICE & EVERYTHING NICE.

TAKE A MOMENT EACH MORNING TO NOTICE YOUR SENSES. Do you see a picture on your wall or a cloud in the sky? Are the birds chirping? Do you smell breakfast cooking? How do your clothes feel to the touch? Does your minty toothpaste leave your mouth tasting fresh? It's awesome that you have all these ways to interact with our big, beautiful world!

SPRINKLE KINDNESS

WHEN TIMES ARE GOOD FOR YOU,
PRACTICE GRATITUDE BY PAYING IT
FORWARD AND HELPING OTHERS.
AFTER ALL, THEY'LL BE THERE FOR
YOU WHEN TIMES ARE TOUGH!

"THIS IS A WONDERFUL DAY.

I'VE NEVER SEEN THIS ONE BEFORE."

—Maya Angelou

HAVE AN OPEN MIND—

when something seems bad, there might be a
bright side you haven't even thought of yet.

Practice taking a step back to look at the
larger picture. Be gentle with yourself, and
try a little humor. Not everything is perfect or
goes your way, but did anything go right?

LOOK FOR THE BEAUTY AROUND YOU.
Some of the best things in life are the little things
we can enjoy with our senses. It can be lying on
the grass, watching butterflies, or hearing your favorite
song. Or indulging in a sweet treat!
Soak up these moments of joy.

But 'Mallows know there is another sense we can
lean on that is just as likely to help you embrace the
positive . . . the sense of WONDER! There's a whole
universe out there to marvel at, from the smallest
subatomic particle, to galaxies beyond, to life in all
its amazing forms—squish on that! Awe-inspiring!

"ONE SMALL POSITIVE
THOUGHT CAN CHANGE
YOUR WHOLE DAY."

—Zig Ziglar

TRY A VISUAL CUE—like a pretty pebble, a handmade bracelet, or even a phone background— that will remind you to think about positivity and gratitude when things get rough.

Keeping a picture in your head is a great way to take control of your thoughts. If you feel negativity coming on, picture a big red STOP sign. Is this thought helpful? If not, tell it to turn around and go back to where it came from!

KEEP A GRATITUDE JOURNAL—write down things that you are grateful for every day. It can be big or small, broad or very specific. Then take a minute to read what you wrote. Even during difficult times, we all have something in our lives to be grateful for. You can also try a gratitude JAR or a gratitude BOX (or a gratitude TOP HAT, if you're feeling fancy), where you write down things you're grateful for on slips of paper and keep them inside. Wherever you decide to store your gratitude, taking a few moments each day to appreciate and celebrate the good things is one of the easiest ways to embrace positivity.

WRITE DOWN FIVE THINGS
YOU ARE GRATEFUL FOR.

1. A *person* you love having in your life:

   _____

   _____

2. A *place* you are grateful you can go to:

   _____

   _____

3. A part of your *body* that makes you feel strong:

   _____

   _____

4. Something that made you *smile* today:

   _____

   _____

5. Something you are *excited* to do in the future:

   _____

THERE ARE SO MANY AMAZING SURPRISES ON THE PATH TO AWESOMENESS.

When you go after what you love, more good things are certain to come along! One of Benny's favorite things is taking photographs with his woodland friends. Can you solve the maze and help him find his camera? Enjoy the twists, turns, and wonders he sees on the journey to his goal.

FINISH

START

Give yourself permission to have fun!

Draw up a "Have Fun!" ticket and give it to yourself when you're not at your best.

LET YOURSELF BE SILLY.

Wear mismatched socks. We guarantee you will
be asked about them. Make up a wild story to
tell, and let everyone in on the joke.

Watch a movie with a friend, keeping the volume off.
Make up your own dialog and turn any drama
into a comedy.

HI, I'M MAUI!

Sometimes Maui gets anxious and scared, but she is determined to face her fears. She tries to do one thing every day that she is afraid of—and usually once she tries it, it's not as bad as she imagined. Doodling can be a great way to express our emotions and plan how to manage them. Challenge yourself to try something new and break out of your comfort zone!

Maui has conquered her fear of roller coasters and wants to check skateboarding off her list. Grab a pen, and help her finish this board.

Draw three things that scare you, and list ways you can overcome them.

THERE'S ONLY ONE YOU,

AND

YOU. ARE. MAGICAL.

GET
Motivated

Just like Jaelyn the axolotl, you're always juggling.
But instead of juggling scarves, pins, or candy bars,
you're juggling all the pieces of a busy, awesome
life! Making space for school, work, friends, family,
hobbies, and everything in between can be low-key
exhausting, and sometimes it feels like there's just no
way to manage it. But we've got ideas that can help
you keep all those plates spinning. Don't worry—
you've got this! After all, you are the alpha, omega,
and all the other Greek letters that make up your life.

PERFECTION DOESN'T EXIST,
AND THE PEOPLE WHO LOVE
YOU ARE HAPPY WHEN YOU
TRY YOUR BEST.

If work or school is stressing you out, try managing your time differently. Try this popular method! Pick a task you need to work on, then set a timer for twenty-five minutes. You can DEFINITELY stay focused for less than half an hour!

When the timer goes off, take a five-minute break and relax your inner and outer self. They will both be energized and ready for the next shift.

Repeat ☺

"FOR EVERY MiNUTE SPENT iN ORGANIZING, AN HOUR is EARNED."

—Benjamin Franklin

Keep your workspace nice and tidy. This will ease your mind so it can work at its full capacity, thinking brilliant ideas. If you find yourself saying, "Eureka!" then it's working.

TAKING CONTROL
AND GETTING ORGANIZED
MAKES YOU FEEL POWERFUL!

If you're feeling overwhelmed, make a to-do list.
You may have a lot on your plate, but once you
cross that first item off, you'll feel SO much better. And
don't forget to congratulate yourself when
you finish something on your list!
Get in there and slay those responsibilities.

TO-DO LIST

★ _____

★ _____

★ _____

★ _____

★ _____

★ _____

★ _____

★ _____

★ _____

★ _____

"IT ALWAYS SEEMS IMPOSSIBLE UNTIL IT'S DONE."

—**Nelson Mandela**

If you're having a hard time staying focused, try putting your phone or other distracting devices in another room, or another country, for just thirty minutes.

WHEN YOU FOCUS
ON YOUR GOALS,
YOU WILL GET GOOD
RESULTS!

We live in a busy world,
and it is so easy to
get overwhelmed.

Your time is precious, and
sometimes that means saying
"no" so you can create space
for what's most important.

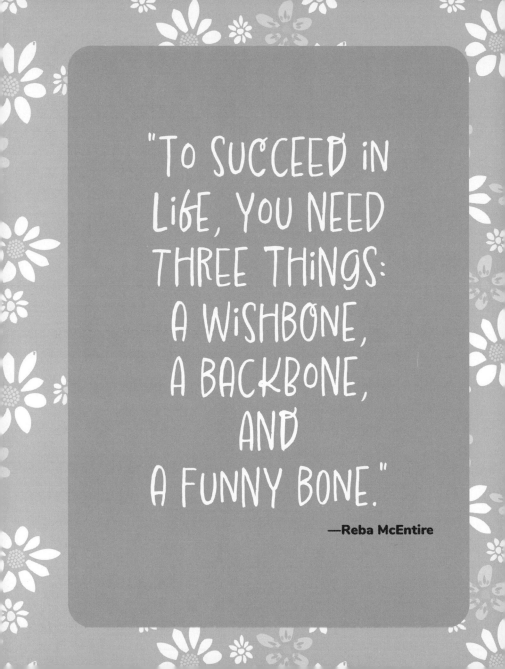

"TO SUCCEED iN LiFE, YOU NEED THREE THiNGS: A WiSHBONE, A BACKBONE, AND A FUNNY BONE."

—Reba McEntire

TAKE A SHAKE BREAK!

(Try saying that five times fast!) But for real, if you're stuck on something, stand up and shake out your arms, legs, and head. If you're getting bored or having a hard time focusing, it'll jump-start your brain by getting oxygen flowing.

Speaking of oxygen, take a deep breath and remind yourself that you can do this.

HI, I'M

Renne the Latte.

Drawing is one of my FAVORITE things to do to have fun. Why don't you take a break and grab some markers or colored pencils and color in this picture?

HI, I'M SID!

Sid loves to listen to music when he is stuck.
Why don't you join him and take a five-minute
song break? What songs will you choose?

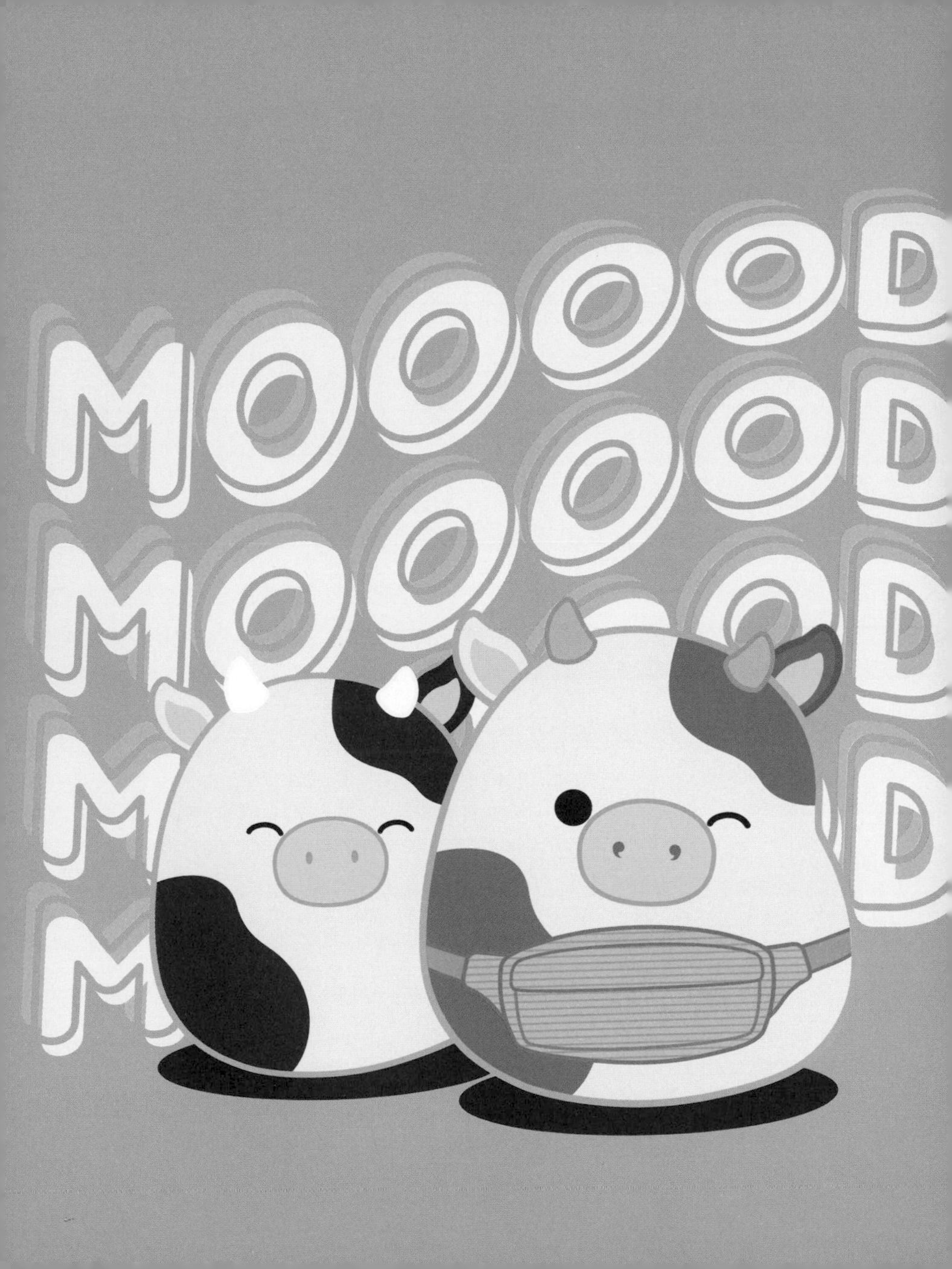
MOOOOD
MOOOOD
MOOOOD
MOOOOD
MOOOOD

WHEN YOU NEED A
Pick-Me-Up

Sometimes life can be really, REALLY hard. As much as we try to stay positive, no one can be happy all the time, and that's OK! It's not good to push away bad feelings. So here are some things that we like to do to get through days when life is feeling tough.

"EMOTIONS ARE LIKE PASSING STORMS, AND YOU HAVE TO REMIND YOURSELF THAT IT WON'T RAIN FOREVER."

—Amy Poehler

Get comfortable with being **UN-**comfortable. Sometimes it's important to acknowledge your not-so-fun emotions so you can feel better. You are a whole person, and experiencing hard emotions is part of life. Accepting EVERY part of yourself, even the negative, is the first step to feeling a tiny bit better.

If you're feeling sad or lonely, let your loved ones know.

Even if they're busy, they'll still want to be there for you—

because you're worth it!

IF YOU'RE NOT AT YOUR BEST TODAY, THAT'S OK. TOMORROW WILL BE A NEW DAY.

Meditation can make you feel better both physically AND mentally. It can improve symptoms of anxiety, high blood pressure, poor sleep, and so much more. If you want to make time for meditation, you can do it anywhere! Just take five minutes to find stillness and not be disturbed. There are even cool apps you can try!

LET'S DO SOME MINDFUL BREATHING.

Inhale for four counts.

Hold the breath for four.

Then exhale for four.

See if you can do that five times.

Then tomorrow, try to do it ten times.

GET A CHANGE OF SCENERY—
and we're not talking about using a blue
screen background. Take a drive down a
new street or to the next town over; shaking
things up is good for your mental health.

EXPLORE

TAKE A THIRTY-SECOND STRETCH BREAK. IT'LL CLEAR YOUR MIND AND MAKE YOUR BODY FEEL BETTER.

TRY MINDFUL LISTENING. For just ten seconds, be quiet and truly listen to all the sounds around you. Are there people laughing out on the street? Traffic rushing by? It's a good reminder to not worry or stress about the future—you're here in THIS moment. Isn't it a nice place to be?

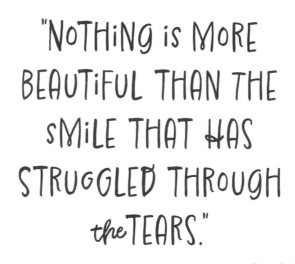

"NOTHING is MORE BEAUTIFUL THAN THE SMiLE THAT HAS STRUGGLED THROUGH the TEARS."

—Demi Lovato

If you're struggling, sometimes it's really good to talk to an expert. Owen is in training to become a therapist. He wants to positively help people feel safe and heard.

IT TAKES STRENGTH
TO ASK FOR HELP—

AND WE KNOW YOU'RE
STRONG ENOUGH TO DO IT.

Wear a Band-Aid when you are going through a rough period. Allow yourself to feel blue, and when you are ready, you can take off the Band-Aid and remind yourself to keep moving.

Let Go

Write in each cloud something
you want to let go of.

YOU ARE WORTHY.
YOU ARE LOVED.
YOU ARE ENOUGH.

YOU ARE PURRRRRRFECT

Everyone gets busy, but sometimes it's good to set aside a night to just be cozy and calm. Rest and relaxation are so important for reducing stress and improving your mood.

Make your favorite snack, and curl up with a good book and your favorite plush. (Wink, wink.)

"THE MOST WASTED
OF ALL DAYS
IS ONE WITHOUT
LAUGHTER."

—e. e. cummings

DID YOU KNOW LAUGHTER CAN MAKE YOUR ENTIRE BODY FEEL GOOD?

Laughing releases hormones that make us feel good, and it makes us take in oxygen-rich air. If you need a pick-me-up, watch some funny videos, or listen to a comedy podcast to give yourself a good chuckle.

GET YOUR WEIRD ON

There's only one you—you're one of a kind, made different, and you were born that way! You have your own likes and dreams and peculiarities that make you uniquely you. And while some of your quirks might seem strange to others, they're part of who you are. And they're worth celebrating! Maybe you like to dip your pound cake in peanut butter and sprinkles, or you like pineapple and olives on your pizza. Maybe you like to wear colors that clash or sparkly pink bowling shoes! Be proud to be different. Let's face it— no one can *you* like *you!*

CELEBRATE YOUR QUIRKY SELF

Write down five things about yourself
that might be a little odd to others but
that are a fun part of who you are.

1. _____
   _____

2. _____
   _____

3. _____
   _____

4. _____
   _____

5. _____
   _____

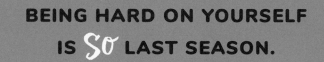

BEING HARD ON YOURSELF
IS *SO* LAST SEASON.

HEDGE-

Everyone knows that Squishmallows LOVE hugs!
But did you know that when we hug, our brains
release soothing chemicals that make us feel calm,
safe, and loved? Give someone a squeeze for
twenty seconds and both of you will feel better.

HUG!

And if you happen to be alone, you can even give YOURSELF a big ol' squeeze. Hugging yourself reduces stress hormones if you're having a bad day. And hugging your favorite Squishmallows doesn't hurt either!

Time for a cuddle break.

"I REALLY THINK A CHAMPION IS DEFINED NOT BY THEIR WINS BUT BY HOW THEY CAN RECOVER WHEN THEY FALL."

—Serena Williams

When things are feeling hard, don't forget to celebrate the small stuff. Think about EVERYTHING you do even in a regular day. Celebrate getting to spend time with friends or making your fave meal. Congratulations—you just took time to create joy in your busy life!

Make a list of times that you overcame something tough—whether it was big, like standing up to a bully, or small, like finishing a difficult assignment. We bet you're even stronger than you give yourself credit for.

THINGS I AM PROUD OF

MEET BEULA!
She loves painting and wants to be an art teacher. If you're having a hard day, try this simple drawing exercise to identify those feelings. Write down the emotion you are experiencing. I am

_____

OK, you're already killing it. Now, imagine that you're putting that feeling outside of yourself so you can look at it and understand it better. Give the feeling a face and a color, and draw it below!

Look at that emotion for a moment. Recognize it for what it is; acknowledge it. This feeling is a part of you, and it matters—but it's only ONE part of who you are. And guess what? It's only temporary.

The next time you feel this emotion, try this exercise again, and see if you picture the emotion any differently. Your relationship to your emotions may change over time—and we're so proud of you for working to understand yourself better.

TAKE CARE OF
You

Taking care of our own well-being makes us happier, stronger, and more energetic. Loving and accepting yourself is one of the best forms of self-care. Here are some of our favorite ways to feed the body and soul. Show yourself lots of love and each day will be a little brighter!

"LOOK AROUND,
LOOK AROUND AT
HOW LUCKY WE
ARE TO BE ALIVE
RIGHT NOW"

—Lin-Manuel Miranda

**EVERY NEW DAY
BRINGS NEW OPPORTUNITIES
TO BE YOUR BEST.**

Spend time outside.

Sometimes we get stuck working, studying, or staring at a screen all day long. BIG YIKES. Those are the times it's MOST important to make time to enjoy the sunshine. Even twenty minutes outside can reduce stress, and the sun gives us vitamin D, which keeps our immune systems healthy. Plant a garden, watch birds in the park, take a walk . . .

Or a bike ride! (Our friend Charity just learned how to ride, and she LOVES feeling the wind in her feathers.)

Even better, go exploring somewhere that you've never been before!

"EVERYWHERE iS
WiTHiN WALKiNG
DiSTANCE iF YOU
HAVE THE TiME."

—Steven Wright

FIND A FUN WAY TO GET EXERCISE.

Thirty minutes of exercise a day is great for your mood
and your body—even if you can't do them all in a row!
Try taking three ten-minute breaks (We like to take one
walk break, one stretch break, and one dance break!) if
you don't have a full thirty minutes to spare. And if you
exercise during the day, you'll sleep better at night.

"GOOD HEALTH IS NOT SOMETHING WE CAN BUY. HOWEVER, IT CAN BE AN EXTREMELY VALUABLE SAVINGS ACCOUNT."

—Anne Wilson Schaef

DID YOU KNOW THAT CERTAIN FOODS CAN ACTUALLY REDUCE STRESS?

✳ Avocados are chock-full of stress-reducing vitamins B6 and C.

✳ Hot foods like soup and decaffeinated tea are extra calming.

✳ This may seem obvious, but don't sleep on eating your veggies! Not only are they good for you but they're also great for the environment.

✳ Indulge in a little dark chocolate, which may improve your mood and mental well-being.

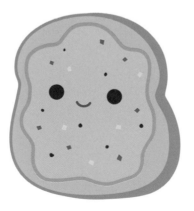

YOU CAN'T HELP OTHERS
UNTIL YOU TAKE CARE
OF YOURSELF—
AND THAT
MEANS TAKING
TIME FOR REST.

We all know that Cam the cat loves his catnaps, and he's really onto something! Even though you're always on the go, you deserve seven to ten hours a night of top-notch sleep. It's essential for keeping your body strong! Even a twenty-minute nap can improve your mood and focus.

* **For healthy sleep, stay away from caffeine and sugar for several hours before bedtime.**

* **Keep your room nice and dark at night.**

* **And find a good napping spot, in case you have to grab a few quick z's during the day!**

HOW TO GIVE YOURSELF
AN AT-HOME SPA DAY

When it comes to being kinder to your body, small things can make a difference. Treat yourself to an instant glow-up with a DIY spa day.

1. Take a warm, relaxing bubble bath. I like to make my own bubble bath at home too. Combine the ingredients below in a clean bowl, then pour it all into your tub as the water's filling up. Step in, close your eyes, and RELAX!

1 cup light oil (you can try almond, coconut, sunflower, or canola)

½ cup honey

½ cup mild liquid hand or body soap

1 tablespoon vanilla extract

2. We like ocean sounds; they make us feel like we're taking a beach vacation!

3. Put on your favorite cozy bathrobe or pj's. Aaaah, that feeling when you hit the ultimate level of cozy.

4. Try a face mask to keep your skin from getting dry. There are LOTS of fun masks that you can get at makeup stores or even your local pharmacy (Some of them even have cute animals on them!), but we like to make our own. All you need is one tablespoon of raw, unpasteurized honey. You can apply JUST that to your face, or you can combine the honey with half an avocado or two tablespoons of plain Greek yogurt. Leave the mask on your face for fifteen to twenty minutes, then gently wipe it off with a warm washcloth. Your skin will feel as smooth and shiny as a unicorn's horn!

5. Sit with your favorite book, magazine, or TV show, and bask in the bliss.

Write down FOUR things you ALREADY do to take care of yourself, and ONE new thing you'd like to try.

MY FEEL-GOOD LIST

1. _____

2. _____

3. _____

4. _____

✳ _____

Social media can be a fun way to connect with friends and your favorite celebrities, but TBH, sometimes it can create bad vibes too. Make sure you practice positive online habits!

Only follow people who bring you joy, and try not to compare yourself with anyone else. Consider the people on your feed—does seeing what they're up to make you feel left out? Or do you feel happy and excited for them? You can also follow accounts that post about things like positivity, gratitude, and affirmations!

✳ Stay in the moment! When you're living your best life with your squad, it's fun to take pictures, but don't get too fixated on getting the perfect post. Enjoy yourself, and stay present so you can maximize the fun.

✳ Keep your cool when it comes to online interactions. Before you comment on something, ask yourself if it's true, if it's necessary, and if it's kind. If the answer is no, keep your thoughts to yourself. But if the answer is yes, post away—your comment will help build a warmer, friendlier community online.

Solution to page 23

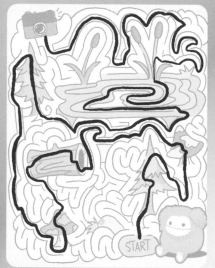

Solution to page 43

SQUISH YA
Later!

So, now you know how to live a Squishmallows life! Thank you for taking the time to get to know us and read our book. You're officially part of our squad of happy, healthy, huggable friends. And remember, you can try out the tips in this book anytime and repeat them as often as you want. Being a 'Mallow is all about doing things your unique, special way! Listen, you are the main character of your story. We can't wait to see what you'll do next!

You're the number one expert on you!

ORIGINAL SQUISHMALLOWS

RADIATE POSITIVITY

Andrews McMeel Publishing
a division of Andrews McMeel Universal
1130 Walnut Street, Kansas City, Missouri 64106

www.andrewsmcmeel.com

24 25 26 27 28 SDB 10 9 8 7 6 5 4 3 2 1

ISBN: 978-1-5248-8232-7

Library of Congress Control Number: 2023940706

Text by Sophie Hessekiel,
Charlie Colborne, Eric Scott
Illustrations: pages 23, 116
by Chuck Dillon;
page 43, 116 by Joe Wos
Editor: Betty Wong
Art Director: Diane Marsh
Production Editor: Elizabeth A. Garcia
Production Manager: Tamara Haus

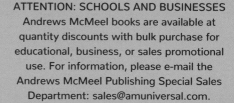

ATTENTION: SCHOOLS AND BUSINESSES
Andrews McMeel books are available at quantity discounts with bulk purchase for educational, business, or sales promotional use. For information, please e-mail the Andrews McMeel Publishing Special Sales Department: sales@amuniversal.com.